The Top 8 Most Powerful Pharaohs of Egypt Biography for Kids

Children's Historical Biographies

BABY PROFESSOR

EDUCATION KIDS

The supreme leaders of Ancient Egypt were known as Pharaohs. They were similar to emperors and kings. They had religious and political power over lower and upper Egypt and were compared to gods. The word Pharaoh stems from a word that means "great house" to describe a kingdom or palace.

The Queen of Egypt, who was the Pharaoh's wife, also was considered to be a powerful ruler, referred to as the "the Great Royal Wife". Occasionally they would become rulers and went by the title of Pharaoh, but most of the time men would hold this title. The current Pharaoh's son would inherit this title and would be required to complete training so that he could become a great leader.

The Great Temple
of Ramesses II, Abu
Simbel, Egypt

The timeline of the history of Ancient Egypt is divided between the Pharaohs' dynasties. A dynasty would be when a family would maintain its power, including handing the power and the throne to their heir.

The Pharaohs would wear a crown that contained an image of a cobra goddess. The Pharaoh was the only one allowed to wear this crown. It was thought that she would shield them by expelling flames at the enemy.

Egyptian tomb

Pharaohs would build amazing tombs for themselves so that they would live well in the hereafter. Generally, it is thought that there were 31 dynasties during the 3000 years of the history of Ancient Egypt. There were many Pharaohs throughout Ancient Egyptian history. On the next pages we will talk about eight of the greatest Pharaohs.

King Menes

Kings Menes is thought to be the first pharaoh to rule over Ancient Egypt. While there is no evidence that clearly indicates it, he was also known as the Pharaoh Narmer. The era of his power is thought to be c. 3000 BC and c. 3150 BC, but that is also questionable.

It is thought that he united the Lower and Upper areas of Egypt by conquest that he founded its First Dynasty and the city of Memphis. In early Egyptology, he was known as the first Pharaoh known by written records. However, as time went on, archaeological excavations did not reveal any evidence of this king and scholars questioned if he did actually exist, or perhaps, was merely a figure drawn from memory of other kings.

After using a crocodile to escape a rabid dog, he founded Crocodiloplis, and founded the city of Memphis which he then established as his capital. He created Memphis after he built a dam on the Nile River in order to move water from the site for this city. He then created administrative buildings, as well as his great palace. This is where he began the practice of sacrificing to the gods and maintaining harmony throughout this land. It is thought that King Menes was killed by a hippopotamus.

Akhenaten

He was born around 1380 BC and died 1336 BC. He reigned over Ancient Egypt from 1353 BC to 1336 BC. While he was more than likely buried at the Amana royal tomb, they were never able to find his body there. It could have been relocated to the Valley of the Kings or even destroyed.

Akhenaten

He was known best for making changes to its religion and he built the city of Amarna. Not long after the death of Akhenaten, the city of Amarna was abandoned.

He was also known for saying that there was only one god, the sun god. He ruled with Nefertiti, his wife, and they proceeded to close several of temples to different gods. He was father to King Tut.

Tutankhamun

He is known to us as King Tut. He was born 1341 BC and died 1323 BC. His reign lasted from 1332 BC to 1323 BC.King Tut is mostly remembered because of his tomb, which was later found full of Egyptian artifacts and treasure.

At the young age of 9, he became the Pharaoh. He wanted to bring the gods back that were banished by his father. He died when he was around nineteen years old. No one really knows why he died. Some theories state that he may have been assassinated, but more than likely his death resulted from a leg wound, which may have occurred due to an accident.

Tutankhamun

Hatshepsut

She was born 1508 BC and died 1458 BC. She was known as the most authoritative woman pharaoh. She was born to Pharaoh Thutmose I. She was raised in the great royal courts of Egypt with two brothers and one sister.

Unfortunately, her siblings died while they were young. She was now an only child. The only male heir to the throne was a young boy that was her nephew, Thutmose III.

Hatshepsut

At a very young age he was crowned pharaoh of Egypt, but she became regent, and she went on to govern the country. She was not only considered to be the greatest female Pharaoh, but also was considered to be one of the greatest Egyptian Pharaohs in history.

Thutmose III

Thutmose III was born 1481 BC and died 1425 BC. His rein lasted from 1479 BC to 1425 BC. He was referred to as "Napoleon" of Egypt and was known to be a great general. During his reign, he defeated many of their enemies and expanded the Empire.

Thutmose III

He was born to Thutmose II and his secondary wife was Iset. He was born as a prince to the Empire. He grew up learning the roles and responsibilities of a pharaoh. His father died when he was around two or three.

He was then crowned as the new pharaoh, and Queen Hatshepsut, his aunt, was his regent. Hatshepsut eventually became quite powerful and took the title for herself. When he died, he was laid to rest in an extravagant tomb at the Valley of the Kings.

Amenhotep III

He was born 1388 BC and died 1353 BC. He reigned Egypt from 1391 BC to 1353 BC. He was Pharaoh Thutmose IV's son and his great-grandfather was Pharaoh Thutmose III.

When he was approximately twelve years of age, his father passed away and Amenhotep was then crowned as pharaoh. More than likely he had a regent that was an adult who ruled during his first years while he learned to read and grew older.

Amenhotep III ruled during the peak of the Egyptian Empire's international prosperity and power. Egyptian culture thrived during this peaceful time period. He reduced the power of the Amun priests and elevated the powers of sun god Ra. This is how he kept his power.

He proceeded to make great alliances with the foreign powers by marrying daughters of the kings of Babylon and Syria. His rule of 39 years was known for its great prosperity. He proceeded to bring Egypt to its highest power. During this time, he managed to enlarge cities and build temples.

Ramses II

Ramses II was born 1303 BC and died 1213 BC. His reign lasted from 1279 BC to 1213 BC. He was born to Pharaoh Sethi I and Queen Tuya. He was named for his grandfather Ramses I.

He was referred to as Ramses the Great and ruled for 67 years. He is known today for building more monuments and statues than the other Pharaohs. When he was fifteen, Ramses became the Prince of Egypt. He also married his two wives, Nefertari and Isetnofret. Nefertari then ruled with Ramses and went on to become powerful on her own.

Ramses II

His father died when he was 25, and Ramses I was then crowned as the pharaoh of Egypt in 1279 BC. He became the Nineteenth dynasty's third pharaoh. Ramses II died approximately at the age of 90. While he was laid to rest at the Valley of the Kings, they later moved his mummy so that thieves would not be able to find it. It is currently located at the Egyptian Museum in Cairo.

Cleopatra VII

Cleopatra VII was born 69 BC and died 30 BC. Cleopatra VII is often referred to as the last of the Egyptian Pharaohs. She would maintain power by creating alliances with famous Romans such as Mark Antony and Julius Caesar.

Cleopatra was born as an Egyptian princess. Her father was Pharaoh Ptolemy VII. She was definitely her father's favorite and she would learn about how to rule the country from him. Her father died when she was eighteen. The throne was left to both her and his younger son, Ptolemy VIII. Cleopatra and her brother became co-rulers over Egypt.

Since Cleopatra was older, she took control as Egypt's main ruler. However, once her brother got older, he wanted more power. He eventually forced her out and took over. Her death is masked with romance and mystery. When Marc Antony had received false information that Cleopatra had died, he killed himself. Once Cleopatra heard this news she became very depressed and allowed a poisonous cobra bite her which killed her.

You can research additional information on these Pharaohs as well as the many others that are not listed here by researching thru the internet, your local library, or ask questions from your teachers, family and friends.

Visit

BABY PROFESSOR
EDUCATION KIDS

www.BabyProfessorBooks.com

to download Free Baby Professor eBooks
and view our catalog of new and exciting
Children's Books

www.ingramcontent.com/pod-product-compliance
Lightning Source LLC
Chambersburg PA
CBHW060615120726
48002CB00010B/2979